Disney Amigurumi

Easy Amigurumi Patterns, Gift for Kids

Copyright © 2021

All rights reserved.

DEDICATION

The author and publisher have provided this e-book to you for your personal use only. You may not make this e-book publicly available in any way. Copyright infringement is against the law. If you believe the copy of this e-book you are reading infringes on the author's copyright, please notify the publisher at: https://us.macmillan.com/piracy

Contents

Belle 1

Alice 10

Ariel 29

Anna 38

Aurora 48

Cinderalla 57

Belle

Pattern Notes

Stich Key

- ch – chain
- sl st – slip stitch
- sc – single crochet
- hdc – half-double crochet
- dc – double crochet
- inc – increase (ex: single crochet inc = sc inc)
- dec – decrease (ex: single crochet dec = sc dec)

- * - complete instructions between the * for the total number of times indicated

Yarn And Hook Size

I recommend using a size D/3.25mm hook.

I recommend worsted- or aran-weight yarn in these colors: skin tone, yellow and brown

Continuous Rounds vs Joining

If desired, you can work these patterns in continuous rounds, rather than joining.

The instructions are written for joining, but feel free to use the method you are most comfortable with!

Other Materials Needed:

- Polyester Fiberfill Stuffing (available at any local craft store)
- Plastic Safety Eyes, 6mm, black (2 per doll)
- Yarn needle (for sewing in ends)
- Embroidery floss and/or crochet thread, black

Head

Rnd 1) In SKIN TONE, make a Magic Circle. Ch 1 and work 6 sc in the center of the Magic Circle. Join to the beginning sc of the round and ch 1. (6)

Rnd 2) *sc inc* - repeat 6 times. Join and ch 1. (12)

Rnd 3) *sc inc, sc* - repeat 6 times. Join and ch 1. (18)

Rnds 4-7) 18 sc. Join and ch 1. (18)

Insert the eyes into the 8th and 12th stitches of round 5, so that there are 3 sc stitches between the eyes.

Rnd 8) *sc dec, sc* - repeat 6 times. Join and ch 1. (12)

Carefully stuff the head, but do not overstuff!

Rnd 9) *sc dec* - repeat 6 times. Join and ch 1. (6)

Rnd 10) 6 sc. Change to YELLOW. Join and ch 1. (6)

Body

Rnd 11) In YELLOW, *sc inc* - repeat 6 times. Join and ch 1. (12)

Rnd 12) *4 sc, sc inc* - repeat 2 times, then 2 sc. Join and ch 1. (14)

Rnds 13-14) 14 sc. join and ch 1. (14)

Rnd 15) 14 sc. Join and ch 1. (14)

Rnd 16) *sc inc, sc* - repeat 7 times. Join and ch 1. (21)

Rnd 17-18) 21 sc. Join and ch 1. (21)

Rnd 19) In BACK LOOPS ONLY, *sc dec, sc* – repeat 7 times. Join and ch 1. (14)

Carefully stuff the body, but do not overstuff!

Rnd 20) In BOTH LOOPS, *sc dec* - repeat 7 times. Join and fasten off. (7)

Use the tail end of the yarn and a yarn needle to sew closed the opening at the base of the body. Weave in ends.

With YELLOW, insert your hook into the FRONT LOOP of the first st of rnd 19, ch 1. Then begin rnd 21.

Rnd 21) *sc inc, sl st* - repeat 10 times, then sl st in the last st. Join and fasten off. (31)

Dress Details (Top Tier)

Row 1) In YELLOW, ch 21. Starting in the 2nd chain space from the hook, *sc inc, sl st* - repeat 10 times. Fasten off. (30)

Dress Details (Middle Tier)

Row 1) In YELLOW, ch 23. Starting in the 2nd chain space from the hook, *sc inc, sl st* - repeat 11 times. Fasten off. (33)

Dress Details (Bottom Tier)

Row 1) In YELLOW, ch 25. Starting in the 2nd chain space from the hook, *sc inc, sl st* - repeat 12 times. Fasten off. (36)

Arms (Make 2)

Rnd 1) In YELLOW, make a Magic Circle. Ch 1 and work 5 sc in the center of the Magic Circle.

Join to the beginning sc of the round and ch 1. (5)

Rnd 2) 5 sc. Join and ch 1. (5)

Rnd 3) 5 sc. Change to SKIN TONE. Join and ch 1. (5)

Rnd 4) In SKIN TONE, 5 sc. Join and ch 1. (5)

Rnd 5) 5 sc. Join and fasten off. (5)

Sleeve Details (Make 2)

Row 1) In YELLOW, ch 8. Fasten off.

Hair (Main Piece)

Rnd 1) In BROWN, make a Magic Circle. Ch 1 and work 7 sc in the center of the Magic Circle.

Join to the beginning sc of the round and ch 1. (7)

Rnd 2) *sc inc* - repeat 7 times. Join and ch 1. (14)

Rnd 3) *sc inc, sc* - repeat 7 times. Join and ch 1. (21)

Rnds 4-6) 21 sc. Join and ch 1. (21)

Rnd 7) 7 sc, hdc, sl st, hdc, 3 dc inc, hdc, 7 sc. Fasten off. (24)

Hair (Bun Piece)

Rnd 1) In BROWN, make a Magic Circle. Ch 1 and work 7 sc in the center of the Magic Circle.

Join to the beginning sc of the round and ch 1. (7)

Rnd 2) 7 sc. Join and ch 1. (7)

From this point on, you will be making the piece of hair that falls down the doll's back and over her shoulder.

Row 3) 4 sc. Turn and ch 1. (4)

Rows 4-6) 4 sc. Turn and ch 1. (4)

Row 7) sc dec, 2 sc. Turn and ch 1. (3)

Rows 8-11) 3 sc. Turn and ch 1. (3)

Row 12) sc dec, sc. Turn and ch 1. (2)

Rows 13-14) 2 sc. Turn and ch 1. (2)

Row 15) sc dec. Turn and ch 1. (1)

Row 16) sc. Fasten off. (1)

Finishing Steps

Use a yarn needle and the tail ends of the yarn to carefully sew the dress detail pieces to the doll's body. See photos for placement if necessary.

Sew the arms onto the body between rounds 11 and 12. If desired, you can stitch the openings at the tops of the arms flat before sewing the arms to the body.

Sew the sleeve detail pieces to the body, placing them from the front to up and over the top of the doll's arms.

Sew the bun hair piece to the main hair piece. If desired, you can insert a little bit of stuffing into the bun to help it keep its shape before sewing it on completely.

Sew the whole hair piece to the doll's head.

If desired, you can sew a strand of YELLOW yarn around the base of the bun.

Use a yarn needle and a strand of BROWN yarn to embroider on eyebrows.

Use a yarn needle and a strand of BLACK THREAD to embroider on eyelashes.

Weave in all ends.

Alice

Stitches

- sc = single crochet
- inc = increase (invisible)
- dec = decrease (invisible)
- dc = double crochet
- ch = chain
- sl = slip stitch
- tr = treble crochet

Indications

- Rounds are worked with continuous rounds technique.
- When working in rows, work through the entire stitch, not back loop or front loop only (unless specified elsewise).
- The last loop to be made at the end of each row is not counted between those indicated in the pattern. You should always add it if not indicated elsewise.
- After a chain, always work from second loop from hook if not indicated otherwise

Tips

- Use stitch markers
- Count your stitches
- Try working tight
- If you don't have the correct yarn size, better to go for a measure less than one more, same for the hook size
- You can find some tutorials on my Instagram account, I will add more

Material used

- 3.5 mm hook
- 2.5 mm hook

- 2.0 mm hook
- Tapestry needle
- Black safety eyes
- Stuffing (poly fiber fill is the best, otherwise some cotton wool will do)
- Black yarn size 3-3.5 (bow and shoes)
- Yellow yarn size 3-3.5 (hair)
- Light peach yarn size 3-3.5 (skin)
- White yarn size 3-3.5 (legs)
- White yarn size 2 (petticoat)
- Light blue yarn size 2.5 (dress)

Note: for a good result, better to respect the sizes of thread and hooks. If you can't, I'd advise you to still respect the proportions between the threads and between thread and hook size (indicated at each step). This way you'll avoid having clothes too thick for the body, and each piece will end up having the correct proportions with respect to the body of the doll :)

Body

Work the whole body (legs, torso, head and arms) using light peach yarn size 3-3.5 and a 2.0 hook.

Legs

Start with white yarn size 3-3.5 and 2.0 hook

R1: 6 sc in magic ring (6)

R2-R13: 6 sc (6)

For the first leg: pull out the yarn and cut it (leave a long tail in case some sewing should be needed).

Instead, after making the second leg, don't cut the yarn; you'll keep on working from there to join the legs.

Torso

First, we join the legs

R14: 3 sc in 2nd leg, chain 2, 6 sc in 1st leg, 2 sc in back side of the chain, 3 sc in 2nd leg (16)

R15: 16 sc (16)

Now we're enlarging to create the booty!

R16: 2 sc, (inc, 2 sc) x 2, 8 sc (18)

R17: 18 sc (18)

R18: 18 sc (18)

R19: 2 sc, (dec, 2 sc) x 2, 8 sc (16)

Booty finished :)

Start stuffing the body

Switch to light peach yarn size 3-3.5 and 2.0 hook

R20: 16 sc (16)

R21: (6 sc, dec) x 2 (14)

R22: (5 sc, dec) x 2 (12)

R23: (4 sc, dec) x2 (10)

R24: (3 sc, dec) x 2 (8)

R25: (2 sc, dec) x 2 (6)

Neck

Now 2 rounds for the neck

R26-R27: 6 sc (6)

Neck done, now we start the head

Head

R28: 6 inc (12)

R29: 12 inc (24)

R30: (1 sc, inc) x 12 (36)

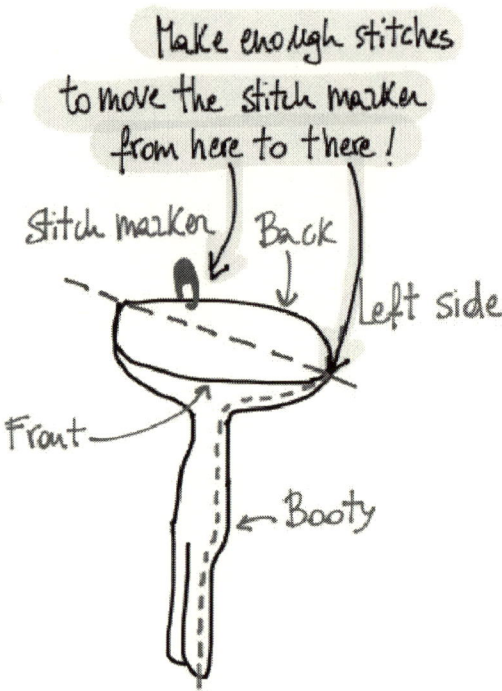

At this point, your stitch marker is probably somewhere behind the doll's back (use the booty as a reference to understand which is the front and which is the back). You must now make enough stitches to position the stitch marker right on the left side of the doll before moving on with the next round.

Why this? Because we're about to give an asymmetrical shape to the head to make the face… if you don't place the stitch marker correctly, you risk to end up with a doll facing left, right, or, even worse, with the head completely twisted around!

If you're already close to the left side, you can simply continue with R31. Otherwise, you must make these additional stitches.

If you're indeed on the back, this operation should not increase the number of rounds on the face of the doll. However, if you were somewhere just past the left shoulder, you are indeed adding one round to the face. It won't impact the look of the doll a lot, you just have to keep in mind to place the eyes one round higher than indicated :)

[I've made 6 additional sc and placed the stitch marker on the last stitch before moving on with the next round]

R31: (1 sc, inc) x 9, 18 sc (45)

R32-R33: 45 sc (45)

R34: (2 sc, dec) x 7, 17 sc (38)

R35-R40: 38 sc (38)

R41: (17 sc, dec) x 2 (36)

Stop and place the safety eyes between round 35 and round 36 8 sc apart. Feel free to modify the position to where you feel it suits at best the personality of your doll. I personally think that placing the eyes very low and quite apart gives a sweeter look :)

If you'd like to make an embroidery for the eyes, that's the best moment to do it

R42: (4 sc, dec) x 6 (30)

R43: (3 sc, dec) x 6 (24)

Keep stuffing while you close the head!

R44: (2 sc, dec) x 6 (18)

R45: (1 sc, dec) x 6 (12)

R46: 6 dec (6)

Cut the yarn leaving a long tail for sewing. Using a tapestry needle, pass the tail through all the loops of the last round, and pull. Make a knot and hide the yarn inside the doll's body.

Arms

R1: 5 sc in magic ring (5)

R2-R10: 5 sc (5)

Then make a slip stitch, turn, make 2 sc, one more slip stitch. This should give you the curvature for the shoulders. You can also decide to stop at R10.

Make 2.

At the end of each arm, pull out the yarn and leave a long tail for sewing

Sew the arms so that the upper part corresponds to round 23 of the body (right below the neck).

Dress

Work with light blue yarn size 2.5 and 2.5 hook

Start by working in rows, the extremities will be joined later to work in rounds.

Row1: chain 11 (10)

Row2: 10 inc (20)

Row3: 20 sc (20)

Row4: (1 sc, inc) x 10 (30)

Row5: 4 sc, skip 7, 8 sc, skip 7, 4 sc (16)

Row6: (7 sc, inc) x 2 (18)

Row7: 18 sc (18)

Don't fasten off. You'll start from here to work both skirt and petticoat

Petticoat

Switch to white yarn size 2 and 2.0 hook

Row8: work in back loops only (1 sc, inc) x 9 (27)

Join the extremities and start working in rounds

R9: (8 sc, inc) x 3 (30)

R10: (9 sc, inc) x 3 (33)

R11: (10 sc, inc) x 3 (36)

R12: (17 sc, inc) x 2 (38)

R13: 9 sc, inc, 18 sc, inc, 9 sc (40)

R14: (19 sc, inc) x 2 (42)

R15: 10 sc, inc, 20 sc, inc, 10 sc (44)

R16: (21 sc, inc) x 2 (46)

R17: 11 sc, inc, 22 sc, inc, 11 sc (48)

R18: (23 sc, inc) x 2 (50)

R19: (ch 3, sc in next stitch) x 50

Skirt

Work with light blue yarn size 2.5 and 2.5 hook

Go back to row 8 of the dress, where you worked in back loops only.

Row7: work in front loops only (1 sc, inc) x 9 (27)

Then, proceed from Row8 with the same instructions as for the petticoat. You should stop a bit before the last round of the petticoat. As you're working with thicker yarn and hook, it will get you several rounds less to do so. I stopped at R16.

Apron

Work with white yarn size 2.0 and 2.0 hook

This part is worked in Rows

Row1: Ch 6 (5)

Row2-Row4: 5 sc (5)

Row5: 2 sc, inc, 2 sc (6)

Row6: (2 sc, inc) x 2 (8)

Row7: 8 sc (8)

Row8: (inc, 3 sc) x 2 (10)

Row9: 10 sc (10)

Row10: (4 sc, inc) x 2 (12)

Row11: 12 sc (12)

Row12: (inc, 5 sc) x 2 (14)

Row13: 14 sc (14)

Row14: (6 sc, inc) x 2 (16)

Fasten off, cut the yarn and leave a long tail for sewing. Use this tail to sew the apron to the dress.

Go back to Row1 to work the suspenders of the apron. In both first and last loop of Row1, make

Ch 9, 2 sc, 4 dc, 2 sc.

Dress ribbon

Work with white yarn size 2.0 and 2.0 hook

This part is worked in Rows

Row1: Ch 7 (6)

Row2-Row13: 6 sc (6)

Tie this stripe with some yarn in the middle to create the bow-shape.

Dress the doll

First sew the apron to the dress. When sewing, Row4 of the apron should correspond to Row7 of the dress.

Then, put the dress on the doll, and sew it on the back.

Using the same white yarn you used for the apron, create a belt for the apron (tie it on both sides of the apron, and then on the back). Using the yarn left from the belt, sew the suspenders on the back. You can cover the part where you sewed the suspenders with the dress ribbon.

Shoes

Work with black yarn size 3-3.5 and 2.0 hook.

R1: ch 5

R2: work around the chain: 3 sc in second loop from hook, 2 sc, 2 sc in next loop (the first one made for the chain), turn around the chain and make other 2 sc (9)

R3: 9 sc in inner loop only (9)

R4: 2 dec, 5 sc (7)

Make two shoes and sew them to the feet.

To sew the shoes I usually do this: I first put the shoe on the foot, and I pass the tail left inside all 7 sc of the last round with a tapestry needle. Then I pull to well fix the shoe and I pass the needle a couple of times inside the feet to fix it. At the end I make a knot and I hide the tail within the shoe.

Hairband

Work with black yarn size 3-3.5 and 2.0 hook

For the band, make chain 10.

The ribbon is worked in rows

Row1: ch 4

Row2-Row7: 3 sc

Tie this stripe with some yarn in the middle to create the bow-shape.

Sew the ribbon on the hairband.

At the very end, tie the headband on the dolls head, passing below the hair.

Hair

Work with yellow yarn size 3-3.5 and 3.5 hook.

You need to first prepare a long chain (main chain) long 17. You're going to crochet one single hair in each loop of this chain.

- First 12 hairs: chain 21, 20 sc in the loops of the chain, 1 sc in the next loop of the main chain

- 13th hair: chain 6, 6 sc in the loops of the chain, 1 sc in the next loop of the main chain

- 14th hair: chain 10, 9 sc in the loops of the chain, 1 sc in the next loop of the main chain

- 15th hair: chain 10, 9 sc in the loops of the chain, 1 sc in the next loop of the main chain

- 16th hair: chain 6, 6 sc in the loops of the chain

These last shorter hairs are the ones you will use to create the bangs. You can add more hairs if needed (you must check for them to cover the entire head circumference).

To add some hairs, just keep working in series from the end of the main chain.

Once you're done, pass a thread in all the loops of the main chain, pull and make a knot.

Sew the hair on the head

Sew the wig at the top of the head of the dolls body (round 46). The 4 shorter hairs should be on the front. Then I suggest sewing each hair but the 4 shorter ones at round 43 and at round 35. 13th and 14th should be bended on the left and

15th-16th on the right to create the bangs. Sew them to keep them in place.

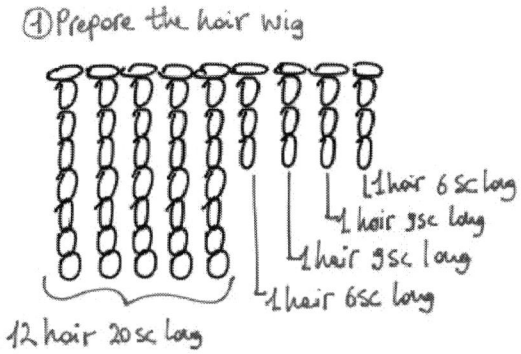

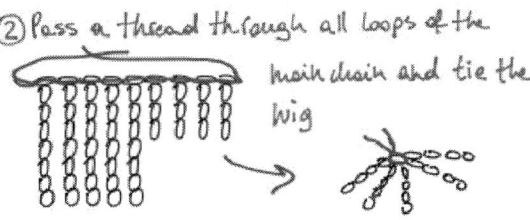

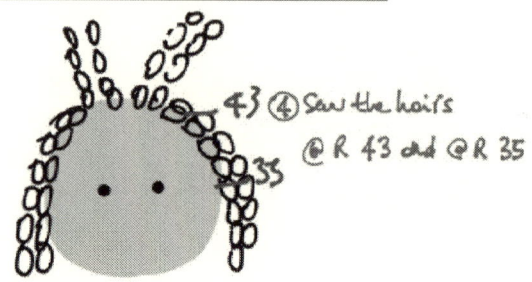

④ Sew the hairs @ R 43 and @ R 35

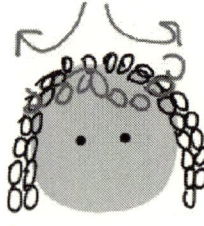

⑤ Bend the 4 shorter hair on the front to create the bangs and sew them

Ariel

PATTERN NOTES

STITCH KEY

- ch – chain
- sl st – slip stitch
- sc – single crochet
- hdc – half-double crochet
- dc – double crochet
- inc – increase (ex: single crochet inc = sc inc)
- dec – decrease (ex: single crochet dec = sc dec)
- * - complete instructions between the * for the total number of times indicated

YARN AND HOOK

I recommend using a size D/3.25mm hook.

I recommend worsted- or aran-weight yarn in these colors: skin tone, green, light green, brown red and purple

CONTINUOUS ROUNDS VS. JOINING

If desired, you can work these patterns in continuous rounds, rather than joining.

The instructions are written for joining, but feel free to use the method you are most comfortable with!

Other Materials

- Polyester Fiberfill Stuffing (available at any local craft store)
- Plastic Safety Eyes, 6mm, black (2 per doll)
- Yarn needle (for sewing in ends)
- Embroidery floss and/or crochet thread, black

Head

Rnd 1) In SKIN TONE, make a Magic Circle. Ch 1 and work 6 sc in the center of the Magic Circle. Join to the beginning sc of the round and ch 1. (6)

Rnd 2) *sc inc* - repeat 6 times. Join and ch 1. (12)

Rnd 3) *sc inc, sc* - repeat 6 times. Join and ch 1. (18)

Rnds 4-7) 18 sc. Join and ch 1. (18)

Insert the eyes into the 8th and 12th stitches of round 5, so that there are 3 sc stitches between the eyes.

Rnd 8) *sc dec, sc* - repeat 6 times. Join and ch 1. (12)

Carefully stuff the head, but do not overstuff!

Rnd 9) *sc dec* - repeat 6 times. Join and ch 1. (6)

Rnd 10) 6 sc. Join and ch 1. (6)

Body

Rnd 11) *sc inc* - repeat 6 times. Join and ch 1. (12)

Rnd 12) *4 sc, sc inc* - repeat 2 times, then 2 sc. Join and ch 1. (14)

Rnd 13) 14 sc. Join and ch 1. (14)

Rnd 14) 14 sc. Change to GREEN, join and ch 1. (14)

Rnd 15) In GREEN, working in BACK LOOPS ONLY, *4 sc, sc inc* - repeat 2 times, then sc inc, 3 sc. Join and ch 1. (17)

Rnds 16-18) In BOTH LOOPS, 17 sc. Join and ch 1. (17)

Rnd 19) *sc dec, sc* - repeat 5 times, then sc dec. Join and ch 1. (11)

Carefully stuff the body, but do not overstuff!

Rnd 20) *sc dec* - repeat 5 times, then sc. Join and fasten off. (6)

Use the tail end of the yarn and a yarn needle to sew closed the opening at the base of the body. Weave in ends.

With LIGHT GREEN, insert your hook into the FRONT LOOP of the first st of rnd 15, ch 1. Then begin rnd 21.

Rnd 21) In LIGHT GREEN, *sc inc, sl st* - repeat 7 times, then sc in the last st. Join and fasten

off. (22)

Seashells (Make 2)

Rnd 1) In PURPLE, make a Magic Circle. Ch 1 and work 5 sc in the center of the Magic Circle.

Join to the beginning of the rnd. (5)

Row 2) ch 6. Fasten off. (6)

Arms (Make 2)

Rnd 1) In SKIN TONE, make a Magic Circle. Ch 1 and work 5 sc in the center of the Magic Circle. Join to the beginning sc of the round and ch 1. (5)

Rnds 2-4) 5 sc. Join and ch 1. (5)

Rnd 5) 5 sc. Join and fasten off. (5)

Hair

Rnd 1) In RED, make a Magic Circle. Ch 1 and work 7 sc in the center of the Magic Circle. Join to the beginning sc of the round and ch 1. (7)

Rnd 2) *sc inc* - repeat 7 times. Join and ch 1. (14)

Rnd 3) *sc inc, sc* - repeat 7 times. Join and ch 1. (21)

Rnds 4-5) 21 sc. Join and ch 1. (21)

At this point, you will be working back and forth, creating an opening for the doll's face.

Rows 6-7) 12 sc. Ch 1 and turn. (12)

Row 8) 12 sc. Do not ch 1 and turn! (2)

At this point, you will be creating six short chains that will fall down the doll's shoulders and back.

Row 9 – 1st "chain") Continuing from row 10, ch 7. Starting in the 2nd chain space from the hook, 6 sc. Join to row 8 with a sl st. Sl st in the next st. Continue to next "chain". (6)

Row 9 – 2nd "chain") Ch 11. Starting in the 2nd chain space from the hook, 10 sc. Join to row 8 with a sl st. Sl st in next st. Continue to next "chain". (10)

Row 9 – 3rd "chain") Ch 11. Starting in the 2nd chain space from the hook, 10 sc. Join to row 8 with a sl st. Sl st in next st. Continue to next "chain". (10)

Row 9 – 4th "chain") Ch 11. Starting in the 2nd chain space from the hook, 10 sc. Join to row 8 with a sl st. Sl st in next st. Continue to next "chain". (10)

Row 9 – 5th "chain") Ch 11. Starting in the 2nd chain space from the hook, 10 sc. Join to row 8 with a sl st. Sl st in next st. Continue to next "chain". (10)

Row 9 – 6th "chain") ch 7. Starting in the 2nd chain space from the hook, 6 sc. Join to row 8 with a sl st. Sl st in the next st. Continue to next "chain". (6)

Your "chains" are complete! To finish:

Row 10) 6 sc up the side, sl st, 3 dc inc, sc inc, 6 sc down the other side. Fasten off.

Fins (Make 2)

Rnd 1) In LIGHT GREEN, ch 4. Starting in 2nd chain space from hook: sc, 2 hdc in next space, sc. Working around the other side of the chain: sc, 2 hdc in next space, sc. Join and ch 1. (8)

Rnd 2) sl st around. Join and fasten off. (8)

Finishing Steps

Use a yarn needle and the tail ends of the yarn to sew the seashells to the body.

Carefully sew the arms onto the body between rounds 11 and 12, over the seashells. If desired, you can stitch the openings at the tops of the arms flat before sewing the arms to the body.

Sew the hair piece to the doll's head.

Carefully sew the fins together at one end so that they come together at a point. Then sew the fins to the doll's body, joining the "point" that you just made with the fins to the body.

See photos for placement if necessary, or place wherever you prefer.

Use a yarn needle and a strand of BROWN yarn to embroider on eyebrows.

Use a yarn needle and a strand of BLACK THREAD to embroider on eyelashes.

Weave in all ends.

Anna

PATTERN NOTES

STITCH KEY

- ch – chain
- sl st – slip stitch
- sc – single crochet
- hdc – half-double crochet
- dc – double crochet
- inc – increase (ex: single crochet inc = sc inc)
- dec – decrease (ex: single crochet dec = sc dec)

- * - complete instructions between the * for the total number of times indicated

YARN AND HOOK

I recommend using a size D/3.25mm hook.

I recommend worsted- or aran-weight yarn in these colors: skin tone, dark blue, light blue, black, rusty orange, magenta, and white

CONTINUOUS ROUNDS

If desired, you can work these patterns in continuous rounds, rather than joining.

The instructions are written for joining, but feel free to use the method you are most comfortable with!

Other Materials

Polyester Fiberfill Stuffing (available at any local craft store)

Plastic Safety Eyes, 6mm, black (2 per doll)

Yarn needle (for sewing in ends)

Embroidery floss and/or crochet thread, black

Head

Rnd 1) In SKIN TONE, make a Magic Circle. Ch 1 and work 6 sc in the center of the Magic Circle. Join to the beginning sc of the round and ch 1. (6)

Rnd 2) *sc inc* - repeat 6 times. Join and ch 1. (12)

Rnd 3) *sc inc, sc* - repeat 6 times. Join and ch 1. (18)

Rnds 4-7) 18 sc. Join and ch 1. (18)

Insert the eyes into the 8th and 12th stitches of round 5, so that there are 3 sc stitches between the eyes.

Rnd 8) *sc dec, sc* - repeat 6 times. Join and ch 1. (12)

Carefully stuff the head, but do not overstuff!

Rnd 9) *sc dec* - repeat 6 times. Join and ch 1. (6)

Rnd 10) 6 sc. Change to LIGHT BLUE. Join and ch 1. (6)

Body

Rnd 11) In LIGHT BLUE, *sc inc* - repeat 6 times. Join and ch 1. (12)

Rnd 12) *4 sc, sc inc* - repeat 2 times, then 2 sc. Change to BLACK. Join and ch 1. (14)

Rnd 13) In BLACK, 14 sc. Join and ch 1. (14)

Rnd 14) 14 sc. Change to DARK BLUE. Join and ch 1. (14)

Rnd 15) In DARK BLUE, *4 sc, sc inc* - repeat 2 times, then sc inc, 3 sc. Join and ch 1. (17)

Rnds 16-18) 17 sc. Join and ch 1. (17)

Rnd 19) In BACK LOOPS ONLY, *sc dec, sc* - repeat 5 times, then sc dec. Join and ch 1. (11)

Carefully stuff the body, but do not overstuff!

Rnd 20) In BOTH LOOPS, *sc dec* - repeat 5 times, then sc. Join and fasten off. (6)

Use the tail end of the yarn and a yarn needle to sew closed the opening at the base of the body. Weave in ends.

With DARK BLUE, insert your hook into the FRONT LOOP of the first st of rnd 19, ch 1. Then begin rnd 21.

Rnd 21) *sc inc, sl st* – repeat 8 times. Sl st in the last st of the rnd. Fasten off and weave in ends. (25)

Arms (Make 2)

Rnd 1) In SKIN TONE, make a Magic Circle. Ch 1 and work 5 sc in the center of the Magic Circle. Join to the beginning sc of the round and ch 1. (5)

Rnd 2) 5 sc. Change to LIGHT BLUE. Join and ch 1. (5)

Rnds 3-4) In LIGHT BLUE, 5 sc. Join and ch 1. (5)

Rnd 5) 5 sc. Join and fasten off. (5)

Hair

Rnd 1) In RUSTY ORANGE, make a Magic Circle. Ch 1 and work 7 sc in the center of the Magic Circle. Join to the beginning sc of the round and ch 1. (7)

Rnd 2) *sc inc* - repeat 7 times. Join and ch 1. (14)

Rnd 3) *sc inc, sc* - repeat 7 times. Join and ch 1. (21)

Rnd 4) 21 sc. Join and ch 1. (21)

Rnd 5) 21 sc. Join. (21)

At this point, you will begin the pigtails, which are six chains braided together (3 per pigtail).

When joining to Round 5, make sure to place your first slip stitch (highlighted in the instructions below in blue) in the stitch right next to the chain—not the same stitch as where the chain started. Then place your second slip stitch (highlighted below in red) in the next stitch. Then start your next chain.

Doll's left pigtail, chain #1) Continuing from where you left off at round 5, ch 12. Starting in the 2nd chain space from the hook, work 11 sc. Join to rnd 5 with a sl st in the stitch that is right next to the start of the chain, then sl st in next available stitch. (11)

Doll's left pigtail, chain #2) ch 12. Starting in the 2nd chain space from the hook, work 9 sc then 2 hdc. Join to rnd 5 with a sl st in the stitch that is right next to the start of the chain, then sl st in next available stitch. (11)

Doll's left pigtail, chain #3) ch 12. Starting in the 2nd chain space from the hook, work 7 sc then 2 hdc, 2 dc. Join to rnd 5 with a sl st in the stitch that is right next to the start of the chain. 11)

You've completed one pigtail! Don't worry about braiding them—you can do that after.

Continue onto the second set of pigtail chains.

Work 3 sl st across the back of the doll's head. Now you will work on the second pigtail.

Doll's right pigtail, chain #1) ch 12. Starting in the 2nd chain space from the hook, work 7 sc then 2 hdc, 2 dc. Join to rnd 5 with a sl st in the stitch that is right next to the start of the chain, then sl st in next available stitch. (11)

Doll's right pigtail, chain #2) ch 12. Starting in the 2nd chain space from the hook, work 9 sc then 2 hdc. Join to rnd 5 with a sl st in the stitch that is right next to the start of the chain, then sl st in next available stitch. (11)

Doll's right pigtail, chain #3) ch 12. Starting in the 2nd chain space from the hook, work 11 sc.

Join to rnd 5 with a sl st in the stitch that is right next to the start of the chain. (11)

You've completed your second pigtail! To finish, you will work the bangs. This will be stitched across the front of the hair piece:

Row 9) 3 sc up the side, sl st, 3 hdc inc, sc inc, 3 hdc inc, 3 sc down the other side. Fasten off. (21)

Cape

Row 1) In MAGENTA, ch 16. Starting in the 2nd chain space from the hook, work 15 sc. Turn and ch 1. (15)

Rows 2-4) 15 sc. Turn and ch 1. (15)

Row 5) sc dec, 11 sc, sc dec. Turn and ch 1. (13)

Rows 6-7) 13 sc. Turn and ch 1.

Row 8) sc dec, 9 sc, sc dec. Turn and ch 1. (11)

Rows 9-10) 11 sc. Turn and ch 1. (11)

Row 11) sc dec, 7 sc, sc dec. Turn and ch 1. (9)

Now you will make the shoulder pieces of the cape.

Row 12) 3 dc, 3 sc, 3 dc. Turn and ch 1. (9)

Row 13) dc, dc inc, dc, 3 sc, dc, dc inc, dc. Turn and ch 1. (11)

Row 14) 4 dc, 3 sl st, 4 dc. Fasten off. (11)

Finishing Steps

Use a yarn needle and the tail ends of the yarn to carefully sew the arms onto the body between rounds 11 and 12. If desired, you can stitch the openings at the tops of the arms flat before sewing the arms to the body.

Sew the hair piece to the doll's head. Then, if desired, weave a strand of WHITE yarn through the middle chain of the doll's right ponytail. Then braid the strands together. Tie (or sew) together with a strand of RUSTY ORANGE yarn. Weave in ends.

Weave a strand of MAGENTA yarn through the top corners of the cape. Use these ends to tie

a bow at the front of the doll, tying the cape together.

If desired, you can stitch pieces of the cape to the doll so that it doesn't come loose.

Use a yarn needle and a strand of RUSTY ORANGE yarn to embroider on eyebrows.

Use a yarn needle and a strand of BLACK THREAD to embroider on eyelashes.

Weave in all ends.

Aurora

Pattern Notes

Stitch Key

- ch – chain
- sl st – slip stitch
- sc – single crochet
- hdc – half-double crochet
- dc – double crochet
- inc – increase (ex: single crochet inc = sc inc)
- dec – decrease (ex: single crochet dec = sc dec)
- * - complete instructions between the * for the total number of times indicated

Yarn and Hook

I recommend using a size D/3.25mm hook.

I recommend worsted- or aran-weight yarn in these colors: skin tone, blue, light blue, and yellow

Continuous Rounds

If desired, you can work these patterns in continuous rounds, rather than joining.

The instructions are written for joining, but feel free to use the method you are most comfortable with!

Other Materials

- Polyester Fiberfill Stuffing (available at any local craft store)
- Plastic Safety Eyes, 6mm, black (2 per doll)
- Yarn needle (for sewing in ends)
- Embroidery floss and/or crochet thread, black

Head

Rnd 1) In SKIN TONE, make a Magic Circle. Ch 1 and work 6 sc in the center of the Magic Circle. Join to the beginning sc of the round and ch 1. (6)

Rnd 2) *sc inc* - repeat 6 times. Join and ch 1. (12)

Rnd 3) *sc inc, sc* - repeat 6 times. Join and ch 1. (18)

Rnds 4-7) 18 sc. Join and ch 1. (18)

Insert the eyes into the 8th and 12th stitches of round 5, so that there are 3 sc stitches between the eyes.

Rnd 8) *sc dec, sc* - repeat 6 times. Join and ch 1. (12)

Carefully stuff the head, but do not overstuff!

Rnd 9) *sc dec* - repeat 6 times. Join and ch 1. (6)

Rnd 10) 6 sc. Change to BLUE. Join and ch 1. (6)

Body

Rnd 11) In BLUE, *sc inc* - repeat 6 times. Join and ch 1. (12)

Rnd 12) *4 sc, sc inc* - repeat 2 times, then 2 sc. Join and ch 1. (14)

Rnds 13-14) 14 sc. Join and ch 1. (14)

Rnd 15) *4 sc, sc inc* - repeat 2 times, then sc inc, 3 sc. Join and ch 1. (17)

Rnds 16-18) 17 sc. Join and ch 1. (17)

Rnd 19) In BACK LOOPS ONLY, *sc dec, sc* - repeat 5 times, then sc dec. Join and ch 1. (11)

Carefully stuff the body, but do not overstuff!

Rnd 20) In BOTH LOOPS, *sc dec* - repeat 5 times, then sc. Join and fasten off. (6)

Use the tail end of the yarn and a yarn needle to sew closed the opening at the base of the body. Weave in ends.

With BLUE, insert your hook into the FRONT LOOP of the first st of rnd 19, ch 1. Then begin rnd 21.

Rnd 21) *sc inc, sl st* – repeat 8 times. Sl st in the last st of the rnd. Fasten off and weave in ends. (25)

Arms (Make 2)

Rnd 1) In SKIN TONE, make a Magic Circle. Ch 1 and work 5 sc in the center of the Magic Circle. Join to the beginning sc of the round and ch 1. (5)

Rnd 2) 5 sc. Change to LIGHT BLUE. Join and ch 1. (5)

Rnd 3) In LIGHT BLUE, 5 sc. Join and ch 1. (5)

Rnd 4) 5 sc. Join and ch 1. (5)

Rnd 5) 5 sc. Join and fasten off. (5)

Hair

Rnd 1) In YELLOW, make a Magic Circle. Ch 1 and work 7 sc in the center of the Magic Circle.

Join to the beginning sc of the round and ch 1. (7)

Rnd 2) *sc inc* - repeat 7 times. Join and ch 1. (14)

Rnd 3) *sc inc, sc* - repeat 7 times. Join and ch 1. (21)

Rnds 4-5) 21 sc. Join and ch 1. (21)

At this point, you will be working back and forth, creating an opening for the doll's face.

Rows 6-7) 12 sc. Ch 1 and turn. (12)

Row 8) 12 sc. Do not ch 1 and turn! (2)

At this point, you will be creating six short chains that will fall down the doll's shoulders and back.

Row 9 – 1st "chain") Continuing from row 10, ch 7. Starting in the 2nd chain space from the hook, 6 sc. Join to row 8 with a sl st. Sl st in the next st. Continue to next "chain". (6)

Row 9 – 2nd "chain") Ch 11. Starting in the 2nd chain space from the hook, 10 sc. Join to row 8 with a sl st. Sl st in next st. Continue to next "chain". (10)

Row 9 – 3rd "chain") Ch 11. Starting in the 2nd chain space from the hook, 10 sc. Join to row 8 with a sl st. Sl st in next st. Continue to next "chain". (10)

Row 9 – 4th "chain") Ch 11. Starting in the 2nd chain space from the hook, 10 sc. Join to

row 8 with a sl st. Sl st in next st. Continue to next "chain". (10)

Row 9 – 5th "chain") Ch 11. Starting in the 2nd chain space from the hook, 10 sc. Join to row 8 with a sl st. Sl st in next st. Continue to next "chain". (10)

Row 9 – 6th "chain") ch 7. Starting in the 2nd chain space from the hook, 6 sc. Join to row 8 with a sl st. Sl st in the next st. Continue to next "chain". (6)

Your "chains" are complete! To finish:

Row 10) 6 sc up the side, sl st, 3 dc inc, sc inc, 6 sc down the other side. Fasten off.

Collar/Sleeve Details

Row 1) In LIGHT BLUE, ch 20. Fasten off.

Dress Details

Row 1) In LIGHT BLUE, ch 22. Starting in the 2nd chain space from the hook, work a sl st, then *sc, dc, ch 1, sc, sl st* - repeat 5 times. Fasten off.

Crown

Row 1) In GOLD THREAD (or yarn, if you prefer), ch 8. Starting in the 2nd chain space from the hook, work a sl st, sc, hdc, trc, hdc, sc, sl st. Fasten off.

Finishing Steps

Use a yarn needle and the tail ends of the yarn to carefully sew the arms onto the body between rounds 11 and 12. If desired, you can stitch the openings at the tops of the arms flat before sewing the arms to the body.

Sew the hair piece to the doll's head.

Use the tail ends of the yarn and a yarn needle to carefully sew the collar/sleeve detail piece above the sleeves and around the doll at the top of the dress. Start at the back/center and work around the shoulders of the doll. See photos for placement if necessary.

Carefully sew the dress detail piece to the doll's body. Make sure to sew the two ends of the dress detail piece together where they meet at the doll's back.

Sew the crown to the top of the doll's head, making sure it is nice and snug.

Use a yarn needle and a strand of YELLOW yarn to embroider on eyebrows.

Use a yarn needle and a strand of BLACK THREAD to embroider on eyelashes.

Weave in all ends.

Cinderalla

Pattern Notes

Stich Key

- ch – chain
- sl st – slip stitch
- sc – single crochet
- hdc – half-double crochet
- dc – double crochet
- inc – increase (ex: single crochet inc = sc inc)
- dec – decrease (ex: single crochet dec = sc dec)
- * - complete instructions between the * for the total number of times indicated

Yarn and Hook Sixe

I recommend using a size D/3.25mm hook.

I recommend worsted- or aran-weight yarn in these colors: skin tone, light blue, white, and light yellow

Continuous Rounds vs Joining

If desired, you can work these patterns in continuous rounds, rather than joining.

The instructions are written for joining, but feel free to use the method you are most comfortable with!

- Polyester Fiberfill Stuffing (available at any local craft store)
- Plastic Safety Eyes, 6mm, black (2 per doll)
- Yarn needle (for sewing in ends)
- Embroidery floss and/or crochet thread, black

Head

Rnd 1) In SKIN TONE, make a Magic Circle. Ch 1 and work 6 sc in the center of the Magic Circle. Join to the beginning sc of the round and ch 1. (6)

Rnd 2) *sc inc* - repeat 6 times. Join and ch 1. (12)

Rnd 3) *sc inc, sc* - repeat 6 times. Join and ch 1. (18)

Rnds 4-7) 18 sc. Join and ch 1. (18)

Insert the eyes into the 8th and 12th stitches of round 5, so that there are 3 sc stitches between the eyes.

Rnd 8) *sc dec, sc* - repeat 6 times. Join and ch 1. (12)

Carefully stuff the head, but do not overstuff!

Rnd 9) *sc dec* - repeat 6 times. Join and ch 1. (6)

Rnd 10) 6 sc. Change to LIGHT BLUE. Join and ch 1. (6)

Body

Rnd 11) In LIGHT BLUE, *sc inc* - repeat 6 times. Join and ch 1. (12)

Rnd 12) *4 sc, sc inc* - repeat 2 times, then 2 sc. Join and ch 1. (14)

Rnds 13-14) 14 sc. join and ch 1. (14)

Rnd 15) 14 sc. Join and ch 1. (14)

Rnd 16) *sc inc, sc* - repeat 7 times. Join and ch 1. (21)

Rnd 17-18) 21 sc. Join and ch 1. (21)

Rnd 19) In BACK LOOPS ONLY, *sc dec, sc* – repeat 7 times. Join and ch 1. (14)

Carefully stuff the body, but do not overstuff!

Rnd 20) In BOTH LOOPS, *sc dec* - repeat 7 times. Join and fasten off. (7)

Use the tail end of the yarn and a yarn needle to sew closed the opening at the base of the body. Weave in ends.

With WHITE, insert your hook into the FRONT LOOP of the first st of rnd 19, ch 1. Then begin rnd 21.

Rnd 21) *sc inc, sl st* - repeat 10 times, then sl st in the last st. Join and fasten off. (31)

Dress Details (Make 2)

Rnd 1) In WHITE, ch 8. Starting in the 2nd chain space from the hook, work 7 sc. Turn and ch 1. (7)

Rnd 2) 7 sc. Turn and ch 1. (7)

Rnd 3) sc dec, sc inc, hdc inc, sc inc, sc dec. Fasten off. (8)

Arms (Make 2)

Rnd 1) In WHITE, make a Magic Circle. Ch 1 and work 5 sc in the center of the Magic Circle.

Join to the beginning sc of the round and ch 1. (5)

Rnd 2) 5 sc. Join and ch 1. (5)

Rnd 3) 5 sc. Change to SKIN TONE. Join and ch 1. (5)

Rnd 4) In SKIN TONE, 5 sc. Join and ch 1. (5)

Rnd 5) 5 sc. Join and fasten off. (5)

Sleeve Details (Make 2)

Row 1) In LIGHT BLUE, ch 8. Fasten off.

Hair (Main Piece)

Rnd 1) In LIGHT YELLOW, make a Magic Circle. Ch 1 and work 7 sc in the center of the Magic Circle. Join to the beginning sc of the round and ch 1. (7)

Rnd 2) *sc inc* - repeat 7 times. Join and ch 1. (14)

Rnd 3) *sc inc, sc* - repeat 7 times. Join and ch 1. (21)

Rnds 4-6) 21 sc. Join and ch 1. (21)

Rnd 7) 7 sc, hdc, sl st, hdc, 3 dc inc, hdc, 7 sc. Fasten off. (24)

Hair (Bun Piece)

Rnd 1) In LIGHT YELLOW, make a Magic Circle. Ch 1 and work 7 sc in the center of the Magic Circle. Join to the beginning sc of the round and ch 1. (7)

Rnd 2) 7 sc. Join and fasten off. (7)

Finishing Steps

Use a yarn needle and the tail ends of the yarn to carefully sew the dress detail pieces to the doll's body. See photos for placement if necessary.

Sew the arms onto the body between rounds 11 and 12. If desired, you can stitch the openings at the tops of the arms flat before sewing the arms to the body.

Sew the sleeve detail pieces to the body, placing them from the front to up and over the top of the doll's arms.

Sew the bun hair piece to the main hair piece. If desired, you can insert a little bit of stuffing into the bun to help it keep its shape before sewing it on completely.

Sew the whole hair piece to the doll's head.

Use a yarn needle and a strand of WHITE yarn to embroider on earrings. Weave in ends.

Use a yarn needle and a strand of LIGHT YELLOW yarn to embroider on eyebrows.

Use a yarn needle and a strand of BLACK THREAD to embroider on eyelashes.

Use a yarn needle and a strand of BLACK THREAD to embroider on headband and the necklace.

Weave in all ends.

Made in the USA
Middletown, DE
25 March 2021